IMAGES
of America

CLINTON

HENRY CLINTON YOUNG. Originally a resident of Iredale County in North Carolina, Henry Clinton Young worked as a lawyer in Laurensville. He helped lay out the first streets in Clinton, thus the town was named for him.

IMAGES
of America

CLINTON

Sam Owens

ARCADIA
PUBLISHING

Published by Arcadia Publishing
Charleston, South Carolina

Library of Congress Catalog Card Number: 2001087137

For all general information contact Arcadia Publishing at:
Telephone 843-853-2070
Fax 843-853-0044
E-mail sales@arcadiapublishing.com
For customer service and orders:
Toll-Free 1-888-313-2665

Visit us on the Internet at www.arcadiapublishing.com

CONTENTS

ACKNOWLEDGMENTS

Thanks to Arcadia for allowing me this opportunity to have a book printed on Clinton. This has been a long task, but it has been enjoyable. There were so many people and sources that went into this book. Thanks to Mrs. Nancy Griffith at the Presbyterian Library for her help with the Jacobs family. Thanks to Elaine Martin at the Laurens Library. Thanks to the *The Clinton Chronicle* office and to Larry Franklin for his help.

I also want to thank Bailey Dixon and Mrs. Georgia Bee Thomason. I know that this has been an inconvenience to my wife, but she never complained about the time I took—especially at night after she had gone to bed. Dr. William Plumer Jacobs' diaries were also very helpful. I thank Robert Vance for his help, and I want to thank Laura Daniels at Arcadia Publishing for the time she took to help me through this.

INTRODUCTION

During the Revolutionary War, what is now Clinton had no living inhabitants. Clinton, the second largest town in the county, grew up around Holland's Store, which was the only merchandising place and post office in the lower part of the county in 1809. About one mile west of the store was an intersection of roads known as Five Points, which attracted many of the men of the surrounding areas with the horsetrack, bars, and chicken fights. Also attractive were the fertile farm lands, which made the area an important center of agriculture, dairy farms, and stock raising.

With the arrival of the railroad in the 1850s, the residents decided to organize a town and choose a name. The name that was selected was the middle name of Henry Clinton Young, a Laurens lawyer and native of North Carolina who had served as chairman of the committee that was appointed to lay out the first streets. The railroad was to prove crucial to the survival of the community. In the years following the Civil War, the town became the home of Presbyterian College, Thornwell Home for Children, and the state-supported institution of Whitten Center. Originally, the area that comprises downtown Clinton was an intersection of two main highways and a local road. The crossing of the Greenville-Columbia highway by the Spartanburg-Augusta highway, and the addition of a local road coming from the northwest, formed a junction of five spokes or "Five Points." In 1852, the Laurens-to-Newberry railroad was scheduled to be built through this junction and as a result, 28 lots were sold to form the core town. Twenty people bought lots for an average of $50 an acre. The very first buildings were constructed between Holland's store and the junction of Five Points. As the little community began to grow, it needed a name for location purposes. Five Points, Five Forks, and even Round Jacket were proposed, but it was finally agreed to name the town in honor of Mr. Young's services. Clinton became the town's name and was so entered on its first charter granted in 1852.

Religion and education came early to Clinton. In 1854, the Methodists came and in 1855 the Presbyterians began their congregation in the community. In 1858 a public school was established and operated until the Civil War. By 1860, although Clinton was still a farming community, the population included a wide array of people.

With the arrival of William Plumer Jacobs in 1864, Clinton received not only an eager young Presbyterian minister but also a monthly magazine for Thornwell Orphanage. Clinton's history can be traced through both the magazine and Mr. Jacobs's diaries from 1864 through Jacob's death in 1917. Dr. Jacobs went to great lengths to describe the fledgling town to which he moved. He wrote that Clinton had a nasty reputation for "gander-pulling, gambling, and drinking, rowdyism, brawling and other little disorders." Apparently, ladies traveling from the lower part of the county refused to travel through Clinton on the way to Laurensville.

The Civil War was still being fought in 1864. The railroad had ceased regular service, and during the last years of the war, the only store open in Clinton was Mr. Phinney's and he was only open on mail days. It is possible that Clinton's streets bore unofficial names until after the Reconstruction period. By 1864, the downtown area contained a variety of stores plus a barroom. Almost every home in Clinton had a loom for waving, usually located in the back room of the house. One lady in Clinton raised silkworms for a time. There was also a male and female academy at this time.

By 1865, after only 13 years as a "chartered" town and a most disastrous War Between the States, Clinton's future looked grim. The general consensus among many was that Clinton was dying. Its poverty-stricken appearance was seen as only a few trees had been planted along the streets. With many of the best men lost in the war, with the post office closed along with many of the stores, and with no railroad service, Clinton was in a severe economic depression.

The year 1866 was an interesting political one for Clinton. The town's first charter expired by limitations and Clinton had to be reincorporated. New elections for mayor and councilmen were held. Also in 1866 Presbyterians started raising money to build churches for the black population and rumors started that the railroad would soon reopen operations. In 1869, with with a population of 450, Clinton had again become an important way-station for the Laurens railroad.

The 1870s marked the beginning of the prosperity and growth that was to continue until the early part of the 20th century, despite the decade being riddled with Reconstruction woes. The railroad again ceased service in October 1870. Violence broke out the same month over supposed election cheating. Citizens armed themselves and the guns of black militiamen were confiscated. Acts of violence continued until October 1871, when President Grant declared Laurens County to be in a state of "insubordination and Ku Klux Klanism" and threatened the county with martial law. Slowly, the population began to decline. The climax of the Ku Klux Klan problems came when 12 members of the Clinton community were arrested and taken to Columbia, the state capitol, for trial. After a long struggle, the men were acquitted and released.

In late 1871 Clinton's streets were deserted, stores lacked customers, and families openly discussed moving away. Knowing that the town was in real trouble, Dr. Jacobs would not give up. In 1872, he began holding meetings in the old female academy for a dime. New people began to move into Clinton. This small growth inspired Dr. Jacobs to announce the opening of a high school in the town. At this point Clinton began to grow and never looked back. The town began to prosper and created a new identity for itself in the South.

One

TOWN SQUARE
AND BUSINESSES

THE SQUARE. This picture shows the square in 1906, looking from West Main toward East Main. On the right you can see a white building, which was the place for people to water their horses. You can see the buggies lining up to get water. Clinton Pharmacy is to the left of center. (Courtesy of Sam Owens.)

Broad St., looking North, Clinton, S. C.

BROAD STREET LOOKING NORTH. This picture was taken around 1906 on South Broad Street looking north. To the left behind the fence is Thornwell Orphanage. To the right beyond the trees is the wooden First Baptist Church, which was torn down in 1909. (Courtesy of Sam Owens.)

M.S. BAILEY & SON BANK. The first bank in Clinton opened in 1886 on West Pitts Street. Clinton residents had very little money, and when Mr. Bailey was asked why he opened the bank when there was no money around he replied, "so I can let them have some." (Courtesy of Sam Owens.)

DOYLE INFIRMARY — CLINTON, S. C.

DOYLE INFIRMARY. Doyle Infirmary was the first building constructed on the Presbyterian College Campus. It was built in 1892 along with the Professors Cottage and the Mess Hall. It is still standing. (Courtesy of Sam Owens.)

Broad St., looking North, Clinton, S. C.

FIVE POINTS. Pictured here is the center of Clinton on Broad Street looking north in 1896. It is the junction of five roads, where the Spartanburg and Augusta highway crossed the Greenville to Columbia highway and met with a fifth road going northwest to Langston Church. (Courtesy of Sam Owens.)

11

FIRST DEPOT. Taken on West Main Street, this photo shows the first depot to be built in Clinton, which was constructed in 1851. It was torn down in 1968 and the building was given to Thornwell Orphanage. (Courtesy of Sam Owens.)

BELL TOWER. This picture is from the Clinton Hotel looking toward the square, c. 1898. On the far left is the CN&L freight depot built in 1851; on the far right you can see the old white building where the horses are watered. In the center of the picture you can see the Bell Tower, which would ring to let the merchants know it was closing time. (Courtesy of Sam Owens.)

CLINTON HOTEL. This 1902 picture is looking toward South Broad from the site where the first brick passenger depot would be built. On the left is the Clinton Hotel, which was built around 1900, and on the far right is the Seaboard Air Line Station, which was built in 1890. (Courtesy of Sam Owens.)

STONE VENDING. This picture, taken c. 1904, shows the Stone Vending wagon in front of Copeland-Stone and Clinton Pharmacy with Mr. Stone on the right and his helper inside the wagon. The Clinton Pharmacy burned in 1908. (Courtesy of Sam Owens.)

L.H. DAVIDSON GENERAL MERCHANDISE. West Main Street in 1905 is pictured here. The building on the left is a pressing club, which later became the snack bar and was run by an African-American resident of Clinton. (Courtesy of Mrs. Blue Boland.)

STREET SCENE. This picture was looking toward the square. On the left is J.I. Copeland Hardware. In the center of the picture, on Musgrove Street, is the Bee Hive Store. (Courtesy of Sam Owens.)

14

PRESBYTERIAN COLLEGE CAMPUS. Presbyterian College is pictured on a postcard in 1914. The card shows Neville Hall and the College Plaza. (Courtesy of Laurens County Library.)

BIRD'S-EYE VIEW. This picture was taken just west of the square, c. early 1900s. To the left you can see a small church, which was the first church in the city limits of Clinton. Named the Mount Zion Methodist Church, it moved into Clinton in 1854 and was located on the corner of West Main and Laurens Streets. A revolving track to turn around engines was located to the right of the trains. (Courtesy of Sam Owens.)

MUSGROVE STREET. This c. early 1900s picture was taken on Musgrove Street, looking toward three stores. On the corner was a grocery store, next door was a barber shop, and located on the end was a jewelry store. (Courtesy of Sam Owens.)

BLAKELY STABLES. One of Clinton's most prosperous businesses in the early 1900s, the Blakely Stables were located directly behind the present location of the Masonic Temple. The Clinton Hotel is on the far right of the photograph. Standing and holding Katherine Blakely was A.B. Blakely, and to his left is Lee Add Blakely. Dr. Godfrey stands behind the buggy. (Courtesy of Georgia Bee Thomason.)

16

GENE'S CAFE. Shown is Gene Bostick's cafe, which was a meeting place for the local breakfast club and would open as early as 5 a.m. If you wanted to know anything that happened in Clinton, this was the place to be. (Courtesy of Sam Owens.)

CLINTON BRICK DEPOT C. 1910. Located between Main Street and East Carolina Avenue, this depot was built in 1908. To the left and on the corner is Briggs Grocery. People came to watch passengers change trains because Clinton was the point to switch trains. Notice that all of the telephone poles are pointed at the top. This was to allow rain to roll off and not soak into the wood. (Courtesy of Joe McDaniel.)

COMMERCIAL BANK. This picture from 1915 shows the inside of the Commercial Bank, which was located on the corner of North Broad and East Pitts Street. This was originally the R.Z. Wright building. Shown from left to right are Homer Henry, president; James Hugh Donnan, cashier; D.E. Tribble at the tellers window; Frank Boland, vice president; and Miss Lois Blakely, secretary. (Courtesy of Sam Owens.)

DILLARD'S. One of four locations where Mr. Larry Dillard operated his clothing store, the Musgrove Street location is seen in this 1922 picture. Mr. Dillard's store had been located on South Broad below the Clinton Hotel. He moved up Broad and opened his business on the east side of North Broad before finally moving to the west side of North Broad. (Courtesy of Owens Collection.)

D.E. TRIBBLE CO. This company was located on Gary Street and was both a building supply store and the only undertakers that served both blacks and whites. It was said that if you attended the funeral, you would help dig and cover the grave. This company was originally built in the late 1890s and is still in business in 2001. (Courtesy of Sam Owens.)

U.S. POST OFFICE. The post office, built in 1924, was on the corner of North Broad and Florida Street. It was replaced in 1977 by a new post office located on Elizabeth Street. (Courtesy of Sam Owens.)

DOWN BROADWAY. This picture, taken in the early 1920s, looks south down Broad Street. (Courtesy of Sam Owens.)

UP MUSGROVE. This picture looks up North Musgrove in the mid-1920s. On the corner is Sadler-Owens Pharmacy, which stayed at this location until 1938 and then moved up four stores. It is now located on South Broad and known by the name of Sadler-Hughes Pharmacy. (Courtesy of Sam Owens.)

JOHNSON ENTERPRISE. This building, located on Hampton Avenue and later owned by Alfred Johnson, was constructed in the early to mid-1900s. (Courtesy of Sam Owens.)

Broad Street, Clinton, S. C.

BAILEY MERCANTILE. This picture shows North Broad Street looking south, sometime between 1875 and 1880. Mercer Silas Bailey had three stores; also on the street was Clinton's last barroom, which closed in 1880. (Courtesy of Sam Owens.)

STORES UNDER HOTEL CLINTON. The Clinton Hotel is pictured in the 1920s, with men seen in front of one of the stores located below the hotel. Mr Jim Pitts had a store; there was also a barber shop and one of the earlier locations of the *The Clinton Chronicle* office. (Courtesy of Laurens County Library.)

BALDWIN'S GROCERIES. The inside of Baldwin's Groceries, located on Musgrove Street, is seen in 1927. Mr. Baldwin is behind the counter. (Courtesy of Brenda Baldwin.)

DAWKINS SHOE REPAIRS. Dawkins Shoe Repairs was located on Musgrove Street and is seen here sometime in the mid-1940s. Pictured is Mr. Dawkins and his little helper, Billy Ross. (Courtesy of Sam Owens.)

SEABOARD COAST LINE DEPOT. The last of the three Clinton depots to be built in town is seen here. It was located on the corner of West Carolina Avenue and South Broad Street. It was built in 1890, and was the last to be torn down—in the late 1980s. (Courtesy of Sam Owens.)

BARBER SHOP. The barber shop shown in this 1931 image was operated by an African-American man named Mr. Crawford. At this time the street around the square—as well as Broad Street—were covered in brick. It was said that in the early days that the horse-drawn wagons would get stuck in the mud and this is how the bricks came to be used. (Courtesy of Sam Owens)

THORNWELL SEMINARY. In 1883, this chapel was dedicated and became the educational center of the Thornwell Home. A course of study was prepared for three departments— primary, intermediate, and college—with room for 150 pupils. It burned in 1904. (Courtesy of Presbyterian Library.)

POLICE AND FIRE DEPARTMENT. This picture was taken on North Broad Street just two years after the city hall, fire department, and police station were combined and moved into one building. Two fireman and other city officials are shown here. (Courtesy of Sam Owens.)

POLICE FORCE. The Clinton Police Department is pictured on North Broad Street in 1937. The double doors enter into the fire department; the door that reads "police department" indicates it as the entry to the police department; and the door to the right is for city station. Pictured, from left to right, are George Holland (chief), Ed King, B.B. Ballard, Simon Pitts, Lewis Bagwell, Henry Young, and Joby McMillian. (Courtesy of Owens Collection.)

COOPER MOTOR COMPANY. The Dodge-Plymouth dealership opened in 1937 under the management of Lynn Cooper and Billy McMillian and was located on West Main Street. This building was later part of Industrial Supply Co. (Courtesy of Sam Owens.)

JOE'S ESSO. Joe's Esso was built in 1937 on East Carolina Avenue for $3,742. Owner Joe McDaniel pumps gas while Carl Crain cleans the windshield. Next door is the building that was constructed by Dr. S.C. Hays around 1930 and later became a Texaco filling station. (Courtesy of Joe McDaniel.)

GILES CHEVROLET COMPANY. Giles Chevrolet Company, located on the corner of West Main and Laurens Streets, was built at the location of the first church to come to Clinton, which came in 1854. After Giles Chevrolet closed, it became the Clinton Newberry Gas Authority. It has recently been torn down. (Courtesy of Sam Owens.)

The Square, Clinton, South Carolina

FIRST RED LIGHT. The red light on a cement column was said to be the first one in town. On the right is the confederate monument. This photograph was taken in the late 1930s. (Courtesy of Sam Owens.)

CITY HALL. Clinton's city hall is located on North Broad Street and houses the fire department, police department, and the city manager. (Courtesy of Sam Owens.)

AUSTIN-JONES. This early 1940s picture shows Austin-Jones Furniture Company on South Broad in the bottom of the Clinton Hotel. The little boy out front is Dusty Jones, son of one of the owners, Bill Jones. (Courtesy of Owens Collection.)

WALLACE'S GENERAL STORE. Mrs. Drucilla Wallace's store, located on North Adair Street, is better known as the official home of the Clinton Red Devil Football refreshment center. Mrs. Wallace provided drinks and candy for all of Clinton High School athletic teams after practice sessions. She was every football player's friend. (Courtesy of Sam Owens.)

CLINTON ARMORY. Pictured here is the old Clinton armory for Battery B of the National Guard. It was built in 1937. (Courtesy of Sam Owens.)

DEPARTMENT STORES. Taken in 1942, this image shows four stores in Clinton. To the far left is Belk's Department store, which came to Clinton in 1935. Next door was Sadlers-Owens Pharmacy, which has been in this location since 1938. J.C. Penny Co., which is the next store, came to Clinton in 1928. George A. Copeland hardware follows. (Courtesy of Sam Owens.)

THE OLD ICE HOUSE. Back in the late 1930s and early 1940s, blocked ice was provided to the people of the mill village by the Ice House, pictured here . If you wanted ice, you would display a sign on the front porch with the amount that you wanted. (Courtesy of Sam Owens.)

THE CHRONICLE OFFICE. This is the *Clinton Chronicle* office, located on North Broad Street. It has been in several locations—West Main Street, South Broad Street, and Gary Street. It was founded in 1900 by Ferdinand Jacobs. (Courtesy of Sam Owens.)

BALDWIN MOTOR CO. Baldwin Motor Co. wasbuilt in 1942and was located directly across from the post office. The Methodist church bought it later and razed it for expansion of their church. (Courtesy of Sam Owens.)

RED'S BURGERMASTER. The old hamburger store, run by Red Pinson for many years, was known to make the best hamburgers in town. It is located in the mill village and still lives up to the old saying. (Courtesy of Sam Owens.)

JACOBS PRESS — CLINTON, S. C.

JACOBS PRESS. Jacobs Press was built around 1914 on East Main Street. It was operated by Mr. Ferdinand Jacobs. (Courtesy of Sam Owens.)

Bus Terminal. Joe's Esso service station was renovated in the 1940s and became the bus station for Greyhound and Trailway buses. There were around 50 buses that came through Clinton every day. (Courtesy of Joe Mc Daniel.)

Rock Bridge Service Station. This old service station is located on the Greenwood Highway across from Rock Bridge Church. Working for her father and pumping gas is Betty Peavy Patton. (Courtesy of Betty Patton.)

HOTEL CLINTON. Hotel Clinton was located next door to the chamber of commerce. This is now the location of McDonalds. (Courtesy of Sam Owens.)

CLINTON CLEANERS. George Bagwell ran the Clinton Cleaners, located on East Carolina Avenue. Next door is the Texaco service station that was run by Gus and Tom Ramage. This is now the location of True Value. (Courtesy of Tops Studio.)

CENTER SERVICE STATION. This picture shows the Center Service Station located on the corner of East Carolina Avenue and South Woodrow Street. The building was originally constructed by Dr. S.C. Hays back in the late 1920s as a home. It was torn down and is now a used car lot. (Courtesy of Sam Owens.)

WHITEFORDS. Whitefords, a restaurant located on South Broad Street, was owned and operated by Ray Whiteford. Notice the special for the week. (Courtesy of Frank Whiteford.)

ON THE MOVE. This 1950s photograph shows the crowd of spectators that surrounded the railroad as this church was being moved from North Broad downtown to a new location on Calvert Avenue. The passenger train on the left was waiting to see it pass by. (Courtesy of Tops Studio.)

MARY MUSGROVE HOTEL. The Mary Musgrove Hotel was located on the corner of North Broad and Academy Streets, directly across the street from the Methodist church. (Courtesy of Sam Owens.)

PIGGLY WIGGLY. This is the grand opening of the Piggly Wiggly grocery store that was located on Laurens Street. Handing the keys over to the grand prize winner was the owner, Joe Holland. (Courtesy of *The Clinton Chronicle*.)

MECHANICS ON DUTY. Pictured is the inside of Cooper's Plymouth-Dodge repair shop located on West Main Street in the early 1940s; it later became the Industrial Supply Company. (Courtesy of Lynn Cooper Jr.)

UTOPIA BUILDING. After complete renovation, the Utopia Building is certainly one of the most beautiful buildings in our town. Hoyt Hanvey is the owner and one of Clinton's jewelers. This building is located on Musgrove Street. (Courtesy of Sam Owens Collection.)

CONFEDERATE MONUMENT. This monument, located in the heart of the town square, was unveiled in 1911 on Robert E. Lee's birthday. The Daughters of the Confederacy helped obtain the monument and dedicated it in memory of Stephen D. Lee, a cousin of one of the daughters. (Courtesy of Sam Owens.)

Two

HOMES IN AND AROUND CLINTON

DAVIDSON HOUSE. Erected in the 1820s, the Davidson house on Musgrove Street is the second oldest house in Clinton. George Henry Davidson, the first Davidson on record to come to the village of Clinton, was the son of Capt. John Davidson of Charleston, South Carolina. The property remained in the Davidson family until 1942. Thomas Richard Owens ("Uncle Tommy") owned the house then. (Courtesy of Sam Owens.)

BLAKELY SLOAN HOME. In 1894, D.E. Tribble built this house, a one-story frame house on Musgrove Street. It was later owned by one of his business partners, Blakely Sloan. This house is marked today as the 1922 birthplace of Eugene Blakely Sloan II. (Courtesy of Sam Owens.)

OLD GRIFFIN HOUSE. Will Griffin or his father is thought to have built this house, located on Centennial Street, in the late 1800s. The outside is covered with brick, and it has large windows and a front stoop to balance the two stories. (Courtesy of Sam Owens.)

HOME OF PEACE. Thornwell Home for Children began when a 10-year-old fatherless boy came to Dr. William Plumer Jacobs' home with 50 ¢. Three years later, in 1875, the first building of Thornwell Orphanage opened and took in eight orphaned boys and girls. (Courtesy of Thornwell Orphanage.)

LAFAYETTE YOUNG HOUSE. The Lafayette Young House is located on the old Milton Road, one of the oldest trade routes through the county. Near the end of the Confederacy, Pres. Jefferson Davis, his cabinet, and an escort arrived in Laurens County and chose the Young House as the President's home for one night. (Courtesy of Sam Owens.)

FRAMPTON HALL. Originally built as the Mary Musgrove Hotel, this building was later auctioned off and bought by the Presbyterian Home of South Carolina. It was made into an extension of the home and is called Frampton Hall. (Courtesy of Sam Owens.)

FERDINAND JACOBS HOME. This house was located on Calvert Avenue and was believed to have been built at the turn of the century. It was the home of Ferdinand Jacobs. (Courtesy of Sam Owens.)

MCCRARY HOUSE. During the late 1800s, a cottage-type house was built on one of Clinton's main roads under two giant oak trees. The building was probably constructed by Dr. Theodore J. Peake's family. (Courtesy of Sam Owens.)

BELFAST. Belfast is one of the oldest and best preserved landmarks in South Carolina's piedmont region and is located in lower Laurens County. The tall Georgian manor house, constructed in 1786 of brick that was made in Ireland, has been a showplace for almost two centuries. (Courtesy of Sam Owens.)

GRIFFIN HOUSE. The Griffin house is located three miles outside of Clinton on State Highway 72. Maj. William Dunlap built it between 1840 and 1845 for his daughter Margaret, who was married to Frank Griffin. Frank Griffin was killed near Richmond during the War Between the States. (Courtesy of Sam Owens.)

R.N.S. YOUNG HOUSE. Located at 508 South Broad Street, this is probably the oldest house in Clinton. It has been in the same location and has been owned by the same family since it was built by Robert Newton Spires Young in 1848. Mr. Young gave land for the location of the college and requested that the main building be constructed so that it would face the front door of his home. (Courtesy of Sam Owens.)

44

THACKSTON HOME. Located on South Owens Street, this home was built before the turn of the century. It is now owned by Mr. and Mrs. Drew Trammell. (Courtesy of Sam Owens.)

RANDOLPH LITTLE HOUSE. Randolph Little built this house beneath a giant shade tree at 600 North Broad Street. The house, believed to have been constructed around 1862, has solid heart-to-pine beams supporting the original six rooms. (Courtesy of Sam Owens.)

POOLE HOUSE. J.S. Poole and Mrs. Allen Poole have supplied the information on this old building, which is presently the home of Joseph S. and Frances Todd Poole. The house is located in the Scuffletown Township, about three miles from Clinton. The date 1818 is carved in a log that is connected to the framework of the front door. (Courtesy of Sam Owens.)

THORNWELL MEMORIAL CHAPEL In 1906 after the Thornwell Seminary was burned, the Thornwell Memorial Chapel was built. It served Thornwell Orphanage until 1966 and was then replaced by the Hartness-Thornwell Memorial Presbyterian Church. (Courtesy of Thornwell Orphanage.)

THE BOWEN HOUSE. People who have lived in the house at 29 Academy Street seem to have a strong affection for the builder, Mr. Bowen, whose initials are unknown. It was built in the late 1800s. (Courtesy of Sam Owens.)

M.S. BAILEY HOME. This home was built by M.S. Bailey on West Pitts Street in the late 1800s and was later occupied by George Cornelson. It was torn down and is the present location of the Clinton Credit Union. (Courtesy of Sam Owens.)

WILLIAM PLUMER JACOBS HOME. In 1882, William Plumer Jacobs built this house on the corner of South Broad Street and East Centennial. Several orphans remained in this location until 1928. (Courtesy of Thornwell Orphanage.)

WILL BAILEY HOME. In 1892, land was purchased from the McKelvey's estate and Will Bailey built this house. At the present time, Mr. Robert Vance is the owner and it is located on South Broad Street. (Courtesy of Robert Vance.)

C.C. BAILEY HOME. This house is located on North Broad Street and was owned by C.C. Bailey. Later, this home was purchased by Collie Anderson. It was built around the turn of the century. (Courtesy of Sam Owens.)

THE GEORGE R. BLALOCK HOME. This home was built by Mr. Oxley who later sold it to Dr. George Blalock. Dr. Blalock was the owner of Blalock Clinic and stayed in this house until his death. It is located on South Broad Street. (Courtesy of Sam Owens.)

THE JAMES MILTON PITTS HOME. The James Milton Pitts Home was located on East Carolina Avenue in Clinton. It was built around 1898. (Courtesy of Sam Owens.)

D.E. TRIBBLE HOME. The "Big House," as it was known, was completed about 1905. It was built in the Victorian style of the day but has less "gingerbread" decoration than most. (Courtesy of Sam Owens.)

THE BALDWIN HOME. Located where Highway 72 and Highway 39 fork, this property is known as Baldwin Heights. The house was originally built by Dr. Spenser around 1919. Later the house was purchased by the Baldwin family; they still own it today. (Courtesy of Sam Owens.)

THE YOUNG HOME. Located on a busy highway between Clinton and Joanna is a two-story frame house that was built before the Revolutionary War. The land was granted to Ainsworth Middleton in 1771. A porch stretches across the bottom level, and there is a lean-to in the back of the house. (Courtesy of Sam Owens.)

P.S. Bailey Home. Mr. Bailey lived on the corner of West Main and Laurens for many years until he built this house on South Woodrow Street. He was living there at the time of his death in 1958. (Courtesy of Sam Owens.)

Frank Whiteford Home. Frank Whiteford, known to many people as Colonel Sanders—the Kentucky Fried Chicken Man—built this home on the Chappels Highway. This is one of Clinton's most beautiful homes. (Courtesy of Frank Whiteford.)

GEORGIA BEE BLAKELY THOMASON'S HOUSE. This house was built around the turn of the century by Henry Young. It is located on South Broad Street. At the present time, Mrs. Georgia Bee Thomason lives here. (Courtesy of Sam Owens.)

LOG CABIN HOME. This is a picture of an old log cabin that stood on Ring Road and was unoccupied for many years. The cabin was said to have been used by the caretaker for Rosement Cemetery at one time. (Courtesy of Sam Owens.)

PRESIDENT'S HOME AT THORNWELL ORPHANAGE. The President's Home was funded by gifts from the estate of Mr. T.J. Harper of Columbia, South Carolina. It replaced the former home of the first president, Dr. William Plumer Jacobs, and has served all presidents since then. It was built in 1928. (Courtesy of Thornwell Orphanage.)

PRESBYTERIAN HOME OF SOUTH CAROLINA. This is one of the Presbyterian Homes of South Carolina, located just inside the city limits on the Spartanburg Highway. (Courtesy of Sam Owens.)

PRESBYTERIAN COLLEGE PRESIDENT'S HOME. Mr. Robert Newton Spires Young, who was instrumental in giving property for building the campus of Presbyterian College, has a son who built a brick home next to his father's. He later left it to Presbyterian College to be used as the President's Home. (Courtesy of Owens Collection.)

FERGUSON HOME. This home was the residence of Ed Ferguson of Ferguson Ford. He ran a car dealership located on West Main Street that later became the property of Gwen Evans Mills. (Courtesy of Sam Owens.)

LYNN COOPER HOME. This house is located on South Broad Street and was the childhood home of Lynn Cooper Jr. Mr. Cooper's father ran a Dodge Plymouth Dealership for many years before acquiring an Oldsmobile Dealership. (Courtesy of Sam Owens.)

THE WHAM HOME. This home was believed to be at least 100 years old. Mr. Wham was the first person to live there, and it later belonged to the Bond family. (Courtesy of Sam Owens.)

J.A. Bailey Home. This home was located on North Broad Street and was built in the late 1800s. Later this home became the Blalock Clinic. (Courtesy of Sam Owens.)

HAYS HOSPITAL. After the burning of the Clinton Hospital in 1927, Dr. Hays rebuilt the hospital shown here in 1928. A house was bought and left intact, while brick walls were built around the original house. (Courtesy of Sam Owens.)

ROBERT BERLEY VANCE HOME. This is the home of Robert Berley Vance, located on the corner of West Pitts Street and Elizabeth Street. It was later owned by Mercer Vance Wise. (Courtesy of Bailey family.)

UNIDENTIFIED HOME. This photograph of a beautiful homeplace was in the Jacobs family collection, but no one has been able to identify the owner. (Courtesy of Bailey family.)

Three

MEN, WOMEN, AND CHILDREN OF OUR TOWN

JAMES FERDINAND JACOBS. James Ferdinand Jacobs devoted his life to many public and charitable enterprises. He was involved in developing their advertising departments of many of the nation's religious papers. He also was responsible for the naming of Maxwell House Coffee. His slogan was "good to the last drop." (Courtesy of Jacobs family.)

WILLIAM "BILL" DOBBINS. Bill Dobbins was from Joanna, South Carolina, and he had an insurance agency in Clinton for many years. Mr. Dobbins was honored when the State of South Carolina named Highway 76 toward Laurens as William Dobbins Highway. (Courtesy of Sam Owens.)

PICNIC TIME AT CLINTON MILLS. Each fall, Clinton Mills would honor employees by having fun and games along with refreshments for everyone. (Courtesy of Sam Owens.)

COACH KEITH RICHARDSON. Keith Richardson is a football legend in Clinton. He came to Clinton in 1969 and remained until the end of 1992. He won 239 games while only losing 56, for an 81% winning record. He won 6 state championships, spent 9 years as Upper State Champs, won 16 conference championships, and shut out his opponents 121 times. Mrs. Richardson is pictured here as well, to the right of the coach. (Courtesy of Keith Richardson.)

FLORENCE LEE JACOBS BAILEY. Mrs. Jacobs married Will Bailey and was the daughter of William Plumer Jacobs. She was also one of the first graduates of Clinton College in 1883. (Courtesy of Bailey Collection.)

FRANK WHITEFORD. Mr. Whiteford opened a restaurant on Sloan Street in Clinton, and then later opened a Kentucky Fried Chicken restaurant. He is responsible for a number of KFC franchises and is known in Clinton as Colonel Sanders. It is obvious from this picture why this is his nickname. (Courtesy of Frank Whiteford.)

WILLIAM PLUMER JACOBS. William Plumer Jacobs was from Charleston and came to Clinton in 1864 to become pastor of Presbyterian Church. Dr. Jacobs restarted the public schools after the Civil War and was also the founder of Presbyterian College and the Thornwell Home for Children. (Courtesy of Thornwell Orphanage.)

SAMUEL P. FULTON. Samuel P. Fulton was a student at Thornwell Home for Children, and he later became a missionary to Japan. He graduated from Thornwell in the class of 1844. (Courtesy of Thornwell Orphanage.)

THE VANCE CHILDREN. Pictured are the children of Mr. and Mrs. Robert Vance. Robert Jr. shows his fifth birthday sign, Russell Gray shows his third birthday sign, and Mary Bailey shows her seventh birthday sign. (Courtesy of Mrs. Robert Vance.)

WORLD SERIES BOUND. Clinton's Little League Team won the state and regional tournament and was the only Clinton team to advance to the Little League World Series in Williamsport, Pennsylvania. (Courtesy of Truman Owens.)

BUS TERMINAL. Passengers are seen inside Joe's Esso bus station, waiting for a bus to arrive. There were 50 Greyhound and Trailway buses that came through Clinton each day. (Courtesy of Sam Owens.)

ROBERT PERRY WILDER. Mr. Wilder came to Clinton in 1935 when he joined the faculty at Clinton High School as a teacher and a coach. He retired in 1971 after seven years as Superintendent of Laurens County School District 56. Prior to this, he served 21 years as the principal of Clinton High. (Courtesy of Donny Wilder.)

COLLIE W. ANDERSON. From selling nickel sox to becoming one of the nation's top producers in ladies' full fashioned hosiery, Collie Anderson is truly began on the first rung and made the climb the hard way to the top of the ladder. He was married to Rosa Wilson of Clinton. (Courtesy of Mr. Dan "Tot" Orr.)

BLUE BIRDS. This downtown parade featured the Blue Birds, led by Miss Debbie Fallaw. The Casino Theater is in the background. (Courtesy of Sam Owens.)

CONFEDERATE SOLDIER. Capt. Robert Spencer Owens was captain of Company F, 14th Regiment, South Carolina Infantry. Mortally wounded in action at Fraziers Farm in the Seven Day Battle around Richmond, Virginia, he died on September 8, 1862. (Courtesy of Tench Owens.)

KINARD LITTLETON. A Clinton High School all-around athlete, Kinard Littleton was signed by the Cleveland Indians of the American League. He waves to the crowd as he departs for Cleveland to join the team. (Courtesy of Truman Owens Collection.)

WILLIAM JAMES BAILEY. Along with his father, he opened the M.S. Bailey & Son Bank in 1886. Afterward, his father opened Clinton Mills in 1896. William James Bailey became president of Clinton Mills upon his father's death in 1926. (Courtesy of Sam Owens.)

LYNN COOPER SR. A native of Cross Anchor, Mr. Cooper spent most of his life in the automobile business. He first entered it as a youngster with the old Ferguson Ford Agency. He went into business for himself with the Dodge-Plymouth Agency in 1937. His son, Lynn Jr., now owns and operates Lynn Cooper Motors. (Courtesy of Lynn Cooper Jr..)

CLINTON CITY COUNCIL. This is a picture of Clinton City Council from 1942 to 1944. From left to right are J.W. Hedspath, Pet B. Adair, J.F. Jacobs Jr., D.C. Huestess, Mayor P.S. Bailey, Frank M. Boland Sr., Hugh C. Ray, and C.O. Owens. (Courtesy of Sam Owens.)

CHILDREN'S TRAIN RIDE. This picture shows a group of children preparing to take a train ride hosted Mrs. Eva B. Land, on the left. These were known as "Mrs. Land's kids." (Courtesy of Sam Owens.)

CLINTON LADIES. This picture shows four ladies who were in Washington, D.C., to honor and show support for Sen. Olin D. Johnson. The ladies, from left to right, are Elandor "Snookie" Wilkes, Ann Williams, Mickey Oshields, and Sue Hamilton. (Courtesy of Sam Owens.)

BAILEY PLANT GROUNDBREAKING.
The groundbreaking of the Bailey
Textile Plant is captured in this
photograph. With the shovel is
Robert M. Vance, grandson of the
founder of Clinton Mills; to the
left is George Cornelson, great-
grandson of the founder; and to the
right is Bailey Dixon, also great-
grandson of the founder. (Courtesy
of Sam Owens.)

MERCER SILAS BAILEY. In the fall
of 1865, Clinton pioneer Mercer
Silas Bailey piled four bales of
cotton onto a wagon headed for
Orangeburg, which was 110 miles
away and at the time was the home
of the nearest railroad depot. From
this sale, he started a mercantile
business. He later opened a bank in
1886. (Courtesy of Bailey family.)

A.B. BLAKELY. Mr. A.B. Blakely and his family are pictured outside their home as they enjoy the shady, relaxed atmosphere. (Courtesy of Georgia Bee Thomason.)

THE CAMPBELL FAMILY. Mr. Grange "Toby" Campbell worked for Clinton Mills for 62 years, and this picture was taken at his retirement. Pictured from left to right are (front row) Mrs. Silas "Willette" Campbell, Mr. Grange "Toby" Campbell, and Mrs. Grange (Beatrice) Campbell (wife); (back row) Mr. Silas Campbell, Mr. Terry Campbell, and Mrs. Terry (Delora) Campbell. (Courtesy of Silas Campbell.)

BARBECUE TIME. This picture shows the Fourth of July festivities at one of Clinton's plants. Employees enjoyed these yearly get-togethers. The mill sponsors games, sack races, and greased pig events. (Courtesy of Sam Owens.)

LARRY BYRD DILLARD. Laurens "Larry" Byrd Dillard was born April 18, 1880 to James Park and Margaret Elizabeth Byrd Dillard. He spent his entire life in Laurens County. Mr. Dillard had a clothing store in Clinton that was located at different times in four different stores. He was married to Eudocia Wrenn Hefner. (Courtesy of B.B. Dillard McSween.)

GRADUATION. The Clinton High School graduating class of 1940 gather for a 10-year reunion. Most of the class members were present. (Courtesy of Sam Owens.)

LAWRENCE N. WARREN. Mr. Warren opened the Clinton Paper Box Plant on East Main Street in the early 1950s. (Courtesy of L.N. Warren.)

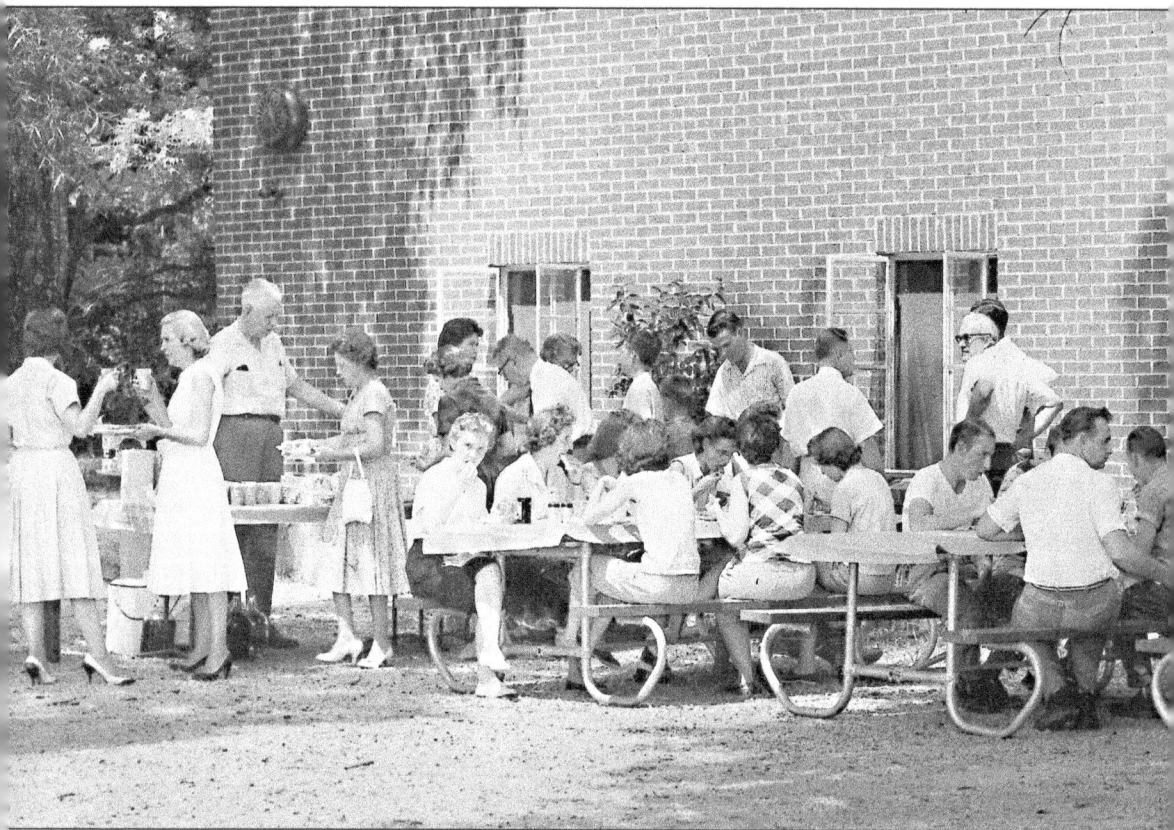

THE BOX PLANT. Pictured is a Labor Day party with employees of the Clinton Paper Box Plant.

RESTING. This mid-1940s photograph is a special picture to the author. Taken on Francis Street, it shows the author's mother, Grace Owens, and father, David Owens. The ice card on the banister post shows 50 lbs., which let the ice truck driver know how much ice they wanted. (Courtesy of Owens Collection.)

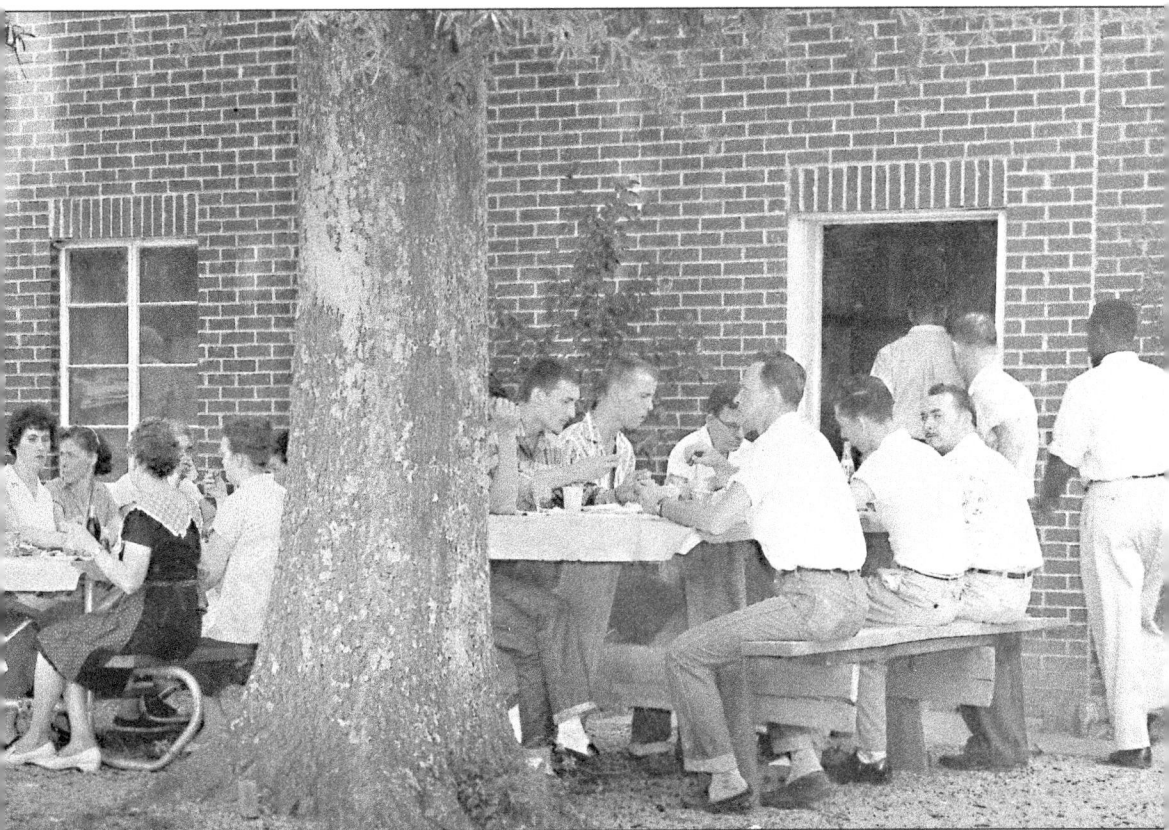

Mr. Lawrence N. Warren stands at the far left at the serving table. (Courtesy of Sam Owens.)

PUTSY SILAS BAILEY. Born in 1904, the grandson of Mr. M.S. Bailey, Silas Bailey was responsible for the growth of many things in Clinton. He served as mayor of Clinton from 1934 to 1946, and was president of Clinton Mills for many years. He opened the Bailey Hospital and gave to many charities. Mr Bailey died in 1958. (Courtesy of Sam Owens.)

ROSANNA LYDIA ABRAMS BAILEY. Rosanna Lydia Bailey was the wife of the founder of Clinton Mills and the plant at Lydia Mills was named after her. She was the daughter of Joseph Abrams, a farmer who lived close by the Bailey homestead. (Courtesy of Bailey family.)

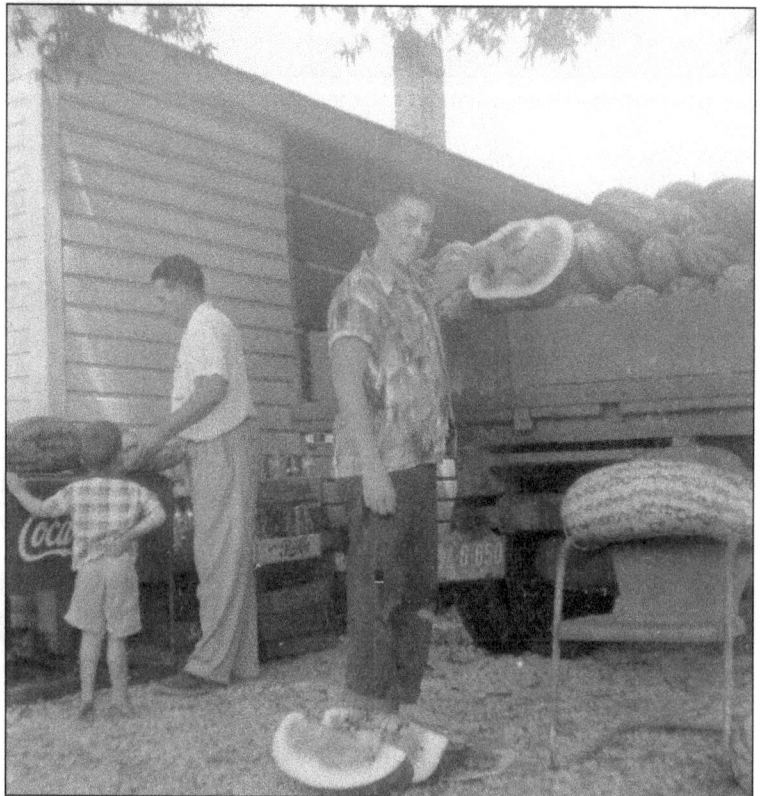

JIMMY DUTTON. Jimmy Dutton (center), son of Braxton Dutton, checks out the load of watermelons. He is helping his father, the owner of Dutton's grocery. The store was located on West Main Street. To Jimmy's left is his father and the small boy is Monty Dutton. (Courtesy of Mrs. Zona Dutton.)

AFTERNOON STROLL. At first glance, this looks like a good afternoon stroll, but for some reason the young man in this picture is riding backwards. The young man is Johnnie Adair, but the girls are unknown. (Courtesy of Joe Edwards.)

THOMAS E. ADDISON. Thomas Addison was one of Clinton's leading citizens. He made his home on West Maple Street. Mr. Addison was connected to the Gulf Oil Dealers. (Courtesy of Sam Owens.)

LAURENS RUSSELL GRAY Laurens Russell Gray was born on March 12, 1898. He worked for D.E. Tribble in the undertaking business before he acquired his own funeral home in 1934. Known as Gray Funeral Home, the business was sold to Ralph Patterson in 1974 after Mr. Gray's retirement. (Courtesy of Mrs. Robert Vance.)

Dr. Thornwell Jacobs Family. Dr. Thornwell Jacob's wife and four children are pictured here. Thornwell Jacobs was the youngest and last living child of William Plumer Jacobs. In 1909, he became president of Oglethorpe University in Atlanta, Georgia. (Courtesy of Presbyterian College.)

Miss Pattie Thornwell. Miss Pattie Thornwell was the daughter of the man for whom Thornwell Orphanage was named. (Courtesy of Presbyterian College.)

Town Council 1896 & '97
Clerk – R. G. Wallace – C. C. Bailey – A.B. Blakely – G.D. Smith – mot
J.a Bailey – A.M. Copeland – Indt D.E. Tribble

TOWN COUNCIL 1896–1897. Shown is Clinton's town council in 1896–1897. They are, from left to right, (front row) J.A. Bailey, A.M. Copeland, and D.E. Tribble; (back row) R.G. Wallace, C.C. Bailey, A.B. Blakely, and G.D. Smith. (Courtesy of Sam Owens.)

MR. LEWIS SIMPSON. Mr. Lewis Simpson was a devoted employee of Clinton Mills for many years, and considered to be very dependable. (Courtesy of Sam Owens.)

DAVIDSON STREET GROUNDBREAKING. The second groundbreaking for Davidson Street Baptist Church included, from left to right, the following: Marvin DeYoung, Arthur Dunaway, Mrs. A.W. Riding, Louie Webb, Alvin Bagwell, and Rev. Clyde Peterson. (Courtesy of Sam Owens.)

J.V. EDWARDS. Mr. Joe Edwards opened a filling station on West Main Street and later built his own station on South Broad Street around 1920. He was a longtime merchant in Clinton with his Gulf Station. (Courtesy of Joe Edwards Jr..)

CLARENCE EDWARD "CHICK" GALLOWAY. Clinton's "Mr. Baseball" and the town's first major league ball player, Galloway was born in Manning, South Carolina, in 1896, and grew up in Clinton. His father, A.B. Galloway, managed and played with Clinton College and later coached Presbyterian College from 1909 to 1917. (Courtesy of Galloway Family.)

CALHOUN FOLK "CALLY" GAULT. A native of Bamberg, Cally Gault grew up in Greenville and graduated from Presbyterian College in 1948. He coached football at North Augusta and won 42 consecutive football games. He later became a coach at Presbyterian College and served as athletic director. (Courtesy of Cally Gault.)

MACK ADAIR. Mack Adair began a clothing store in the 1930s. He moved his store into the previously owned Sadlers Owens Pharmacy located on the corner of Musgrove and Main Streets in 1937. His son, Jim Adair, runs the store today. (Courtesy of Jim Adair.)

GEN. ANSEL B. GODFREY. Ansel B. Godfrey, seen here as a retired National Guard officer, began his military career in 1922 with a commission as a Second Lieutenant in the Officers Reserve C Corps. He resided at 501 South Adair Street. (Courtesy of Sam Owens.)

CASSIUS MERCER BAILEY. Cassius Bailey was instrumental in the success of Lydia Mills, and he also helped to start a grammar school for the Lydia Village. He built a home called Boxwood Gardens, which is now owned by Bailey Dixon. (Courtesy of Bailey Family.)

JOHN CLAY DIXON. John Dixon is photographed with his parents as he signs the contract with Virginia Tech in June 1980. He became captain of the Virginia Tech basketball squad that had the chance to play in Honolulu and Madison Square Garden. (Courtesy of Bailey Family.)

MERCER BAILEY VANCE. Mercer Bailey Vance was the oldest Vance child, born on November 4, 1902. She was raised in a strict Presbyterian family and encouraged to become involved in education. Many people, including her daughter, grandchildren, and hundreds of students, were encouraged to follow in her footsteps. (Courtesy of Robert Vance.)

REMODELING. This photograph was taken after M.S. Bailey & Son Bankers remodeled their bank in 1955. In the picture, nephew Robert M. Vance is on the left and grandson George H. Cornelson IV is on the right, while Emma Bailey Cornelson opens the new areas on May 10, 1955. (Courtesy of Robert Vance.)

CONGREGATION. This is the congregation of the Associated Reformed Presbyterian Church, located on North Broad Street. Mr. Betts was pastor of this church. (Courtesy of Georgia Bee Thomason.)

MEMBERS. Pictured here are the men of Broad Street Methodist Church, located on North Broad Street. (Courtesy of Sam Owens.)

NATIONAL GUARD. A few members of the Battery B National Guards are shown here and are identified from left to right as Arthur Davis, Sam Owens, Bill Bailey, Billy Lowery, Freddie Attaway, Silas Campbell, and Joe Spillers. (Courtesy of Sam Owens.)

ROBERT AND VIRGINIA VANCE.
Robert Vance has made many
contributions to the county
through executive careers
with Clinton Mills, Inc. and
M.S. Bailey and Son Bankers,
and with leadership roles
in the Presbyterian church,
Presbyterian College, and
other charities. He is married
to Virginia Gray Vance.
(Courtesy of Robert Vance.)

WILLIAM "BILL" SHIELDS. Bill
Shields was a longtime photographer
with a studio in downtown
Clinton. Mr. Shields later moved
into Presbyterian Home of South
Carolina, where he lived until his
death. (Courtesy of Sam Owens.)

CLAUDE CROCKER. Claude Crocker was a man that everyone in Clinton knew. Mr. Crocker spent most of his childhood in the Clinton-Lydia area and played professional baseball with the Brookland Dodgers. He was an industrial engineer for Clinton Mills, as well, until his retirement. (Courtesy of Sam Owens.)

CALVARY GROUNDBREAKING. In the mid-1950s, Calvary Baptist Church built a new addition. Pictured here with the shovel is Mrs. Kate Riddle. Behind her, from left to right, are Glenn Downs, Robert Vance, George Reed, Fred Galloway, Clarence Brookshire, and Rev. J.W. Spillers. (Courtesy of Sam Owens.)

98

Four

HOUSES OF WORSHIP

PRESBYTERIAN CHURCH. First Presbyterian Church in Clinton was organized in 1855 and located on East Carolina Avenue. The first building was small and wooden, and it was replaced in 1902 with a Stone Church that burned in 1929. The present church was built in 1930. (Courtesy of Sam Owens.)

METHODIST CHURCH. The Methodist church was the first church to come to Clinton, arriving in 1854. After changing locations, it became known as Broad Street Methodist Church in 1914. (Courtesy of Sam Owens.)

FIRST BAPTIST CHURCH — CLINTON, S. C.

FIRST BAPTIST CHURCH. First Baptist Church was organized in 1881 and was located on South Broad Street. Like many of the earlier churches, it was a little wooden structure. In 1909, a brick building replaced it. (Courtesy of Sam Owens.)

LANGSTON CHURCH. During the organization of the Langston Church in 1773, the church was called the Baptist Church of Christ and was located on land given by Solomon Langston. (Courtesy of Sam Owens.)

LEESVILLE METHODIST. Due to several delays, Leesville Methodist Church was not begun until 1866, when the church lot of one acre was purchased. When completed, it had two stories, and the second story was used for a community hall. (Courtesy of Sam Owens.)

ST. JOHN'S LUTHERAN CHURCH. St. John's Church was organized formally on July 11, 1920, with 21 members. Rev. J. LaGrande Mayer was the first resident pastor. It is now located on the Greenwood Highway. (Courtesy of Sam Owens.)

A.R.P. CHURCH. Providence Associate Reformed Presbyterian Church was organized September 10, 1836, with Rev. James L. Young as its first pastor. A Revolutionary War soldier named William Bill Blakely was the main instigator for the church's founding. This church was built in the town of Clinton in 1902. (Courtesy of Sam Owens.)

HEBRON CHURCH. Hebron Church was organized and located in the town of Clinton in 1883. Rev. G.W. Watson was its first pastor. Reverend Coker became pastor in 1947 and under his ministry the entire church has been rebuilt. (Courtesy of Sam Owens.)

BELLVIEW BAPTIST CHURCH. On April 26, 1900, a new church met with organization in mind. Mr. Lafayette Ramage, who had been raised by his aunt, Sallie Bell, gave one and five-eighths acres for the church to be built with his aunt's house in view. This is how it received its name. (Courtesy of Sam Owens.)

CALVARY BAPTIST CHURCH. Calvary Baptist Church was organized in 1904 on Sloan Street. It burned in 1911 and Clinton Mills donated land on the corner of Sloan and Jefferson Streets to rebuild in 1912. This is the picture of the brick church, which was built in 1942. (Courtesy of Sam Owens.)

ELIZABETH STREET CHURCH OF GOD. This church is located on the corner of Musgrove Street and Frances Street, and has been there at least since 1940. (Courtesy of Sam Owens.)

LYDIA FIRST BAPTIST. The first settled pastor for Lydia Baptist Church was Rev. J.B. Brock, who was there from 1907 to 1909. In 1908, Lydia Baptist applied for membership into the Baptist Association. The Baptist first met in the white church south of the railroad tracks. This church was built on Palmetto Street in 1936. (Courtesy of Rossie B. Hanna.)

LYDIA CHURCH OF GOD. In 1953, A.F. Newport, along with 14 others, organized the Church of God in Lydia. It is believed that the first congregational meetings were held at 74 Palmetto Street. Later, a permanent church building was constructed on Cedar Street. The first pastor was the Rev. Rufus Lee Powell. It has a strong congregation today under the leadership of Rev. J.B. Vanderford. (Courtesy of Rossie B. Hanna.)

PENTECOSTAL HOLINESS CHURCH. The Pentecostal Church in this picture was located on Jackson Street in the middle 1940s. This group picture was taken after the morning service. (Courtesy of Sam Owens.)

THE NEW BETHEL A.M.E. CHURCH. Bethel A.M.E. Church was founded in 1880 and had its beginnings with Friendship A.M.E. Church, located on South Bell Street in Clinton. In 1906, the church, which is now known as New Bethel A.M.E., was rebuilt by Rev. J.W. Douglas as pastor. (Courtesy of Sam Owens.)

HURRICANE CHURCH. Hurricane Baptist Church, located approximately five miles east of Clinton, was founded August 28, 1832, by elders from Bush River. During the construction of the church, a storm completely destroyed the building. In its rebuilding, the church got its name from the storm. (Courtesy of Sam Owens.)

Five

EDUCATIONAL FACILITIES

THE BEGINNING. Clinton's first public school was built on Academy Street in 1858. Squire Craig donated the land for the school, and it became known as the Female Academy. It operated until the Civil War. (Courtesy of Sam Owens.)

ACADEMY STREET SCHOOL

ACADEMY STREET SCHOOL. As years passed, Clinton's grammar school on Academy Street became too small. In 1910, this new two-story brick school was built at a cost of $20,000 to house all students from first through tenth grades. (Courtesy of Sam Owens.)

HIGH SCHOOL, CLINTON, SOUTH CAROLINA

CLINTON HIGH SCHOOL. In 1917, with the school system still growing, the town decided to build a high school to separate the older children from the younger ones. Clinton High was built on Hampton Avenue and the Academy Street school was used as a grammar school. (Courtesy of Sam Owens.)

PROVIDENCE SCHOOL. As Lydia Mill continued to grow, the Bailey family thought it was time for Lydia to have its own grammar school. In 1920, Providence was opened, which gave both mill villages a grammar school. (Courtesy of Sam Owens.)

FLORIDA STREET SCHOOL. This was Clinton's third grammar school. It was built in 1924 on Florida Street. The area now had a grammar school in both the Clinton Mill Village and the Lydia Mill Village, as well as one across town. The District 56 offices are now in this building. (Courtesy of Sam Owens.)

BELL STREET MIDDLE SCHOOL. This school was at one time called Bell Street High School. It is located on the old Lydia Mill Road, and it later became one of Clinton's middle schools, which housed sixth, seventh, and eighth grades. (Courtesy of Sam Owens.)

MARTHA DENDY SCHOOL. Clinton's first black school, it opened in 1928 and was located on North Bell Street. It burned in 1949 and was rebuilt in 1950. Its first name was Bell Street High, but it is now known as Martha Dendy Middle School. (Courtesy of Sam Owens.)

Six

TEXTILE MILLS AND OTHER INDUSTRIES

THE ORIGINAL PLANT. The original textile plant, located on was was called Sloan Hill near Lovers Retreat, opened in 1896. It was called the Clinton Manufacturing Plant, and it was later known as "the little mill." (Courtesy of Clinton Mills.)

LYDIA PLANT. The second textile plant opened in Clinton in 1902 and was named after the wife of the founder, Rosanna Lydia Bailey. (Courtesy of Clinton Mills.)

NUMBER TWO PLANT. The third textile plant built by Mr. M.S. Bailey was located next to the original plant. It was built in 1903 and later became known as "the big plant." (Courtesy of Clinton Mills.)

BAILEY PLANT. This was the fourth textile plant built in Clinton by the Bailey family. The construction took place in 1966, and its location was on the Laurens Highway just beyond the city limits. It was named after the Bailey family. (Courtesy of Clinton Mills.)

CLINTON MILL COMPANY STORE
CORNER SLOAN AND ACADEMY
FACING SLOAN
PICTURE (RUTH WHITLOCK)

CLINTON COMPANY STORE. The Clinton Mill Company Store, built in 1916 and first managed by Joe Simpson, was located on the corner of North Sloan and Academy Streets. It was replaced in 1950. (Courtesy of Clinton Mills.)

LYDIA COMPANY STORE. The Lydia Mill Company Store was built in 1917 and located on Peachtree Street. At one time mill employees used "looneys," which were tokens used in place of money as an "advance" on their pay. (Courtesy of Lydia Mills.)

SOFTBALL CHAMPIONS. The Calvary Baptist Church city softball champions, from left to right, are (front row) Truman Owens, Fred Satterfield, Hall King (coach), Rev. J.W. Spillers (receiving trophy), W.C. Baldwin (presenting trophy), Dennis Robinson, Earl McElhannon, and Sam Owens; (back row) Tom Brown, Pat Lowe, Herb Fallaw, Ed Ballew, Phil King, Bill Cauble, Charles Kinard, Horace Robinson, and Rock McGinnis. (Courtesy of Truman Owens.)

116

ACADEMY STREET CHAMPS. The Academy Street School Baseball Team (of the Clinton Mill Village) were champions with a record of 21–0. They are, from left to right, Mike Cannon, Freddy Samples, Gary Hancock, Charles Huey, Ronald Brookshire, Duck Person, and Terry Campbell; (standing) Bobby Thomas, Jeter Dunnaway, Gilbert Kidd, Coach Truman Owens, David Lambert, Wallace Patterson, and Ronald Quinn. (Courtesy of Truman Owens.)

HOMES ON FRANCIS STREET. These homes, pictured in 1936, and were rented to the employees of the mill. At the time, workers at Clinton Mill were provided with a housing. (Courtesy of Sam Owens.)

HOMES ON GORDON STREET, 1936. These homes were built in the early 1900s; they were all made alike and were practically rent-free. (Courtesy of Sam Owens.)

OVERHEAD VIEW. This 1930s picture of plants number one and two also shows the bandstand and homes near the plants. (Courtesy of Sam Owens.)

TAKE ME OUT TO THE BALL GAME. This was the cry at Lydia Mill Village on each Fourth of July. Everything stopped when the game was on. The field was located behind the Providence School grounds. (Courtesy of Bailey family.)

LYDIA HOMES. Pictured in the early 1930s, these were the first homes located in Lydia when coming from the Laurens Highway. (Courtesy of Sam Owens.)

GROUND CREW. Bit Eustace (left) and Donald "Hard Rock" McGinnis (right) were hard at work before any ball game. They were the ground crew for all textile games, and were relied on to keep the field in playing condition. (Courtesy of Truman Owens.)

Seven

SPORTING EVENTS
AND ENTERTAINMENT

CAVALIER BALL PARK. In the late 1940s, Mr. Silas Bailey wanted big time baseball, so he had this park built to house a semi-pro textile team that could compete with any other textile team. (Courtesy of Sam Owens.)

LITTLE LEAGUE. The Clinton Little League team went to the Little League World Series in Williamsport, Pennsylvania, in 1950. Unfortunately, they lost to Connecticut in the championship game. (Courtesy of Truman Owens.)

CLINTON COLLEGE BASEBALL. Shown here is Clinton College's baseball team in 1901. (Courtesy of Skeeter Galloway.)

FIRST CLINTON HIGH SCHOOL FOOTBALL TEAM. This is a picture of the high school's first football team in 1921, coached by Lonnie McMillian. (Courtesy of Mrs. Shirley Timmons.)

PRESBYTERIAN COLLEGE'S FIRST FOOTBALL TEAM. Presbyterian College, originally called Clinton College, was organized in 1880. In 1904 it was named Presbyterian College. This was their first organized football team. (Courtesy of Skeeter Galloway.)

LYDIA MILL BASEBALL. This was one of the many Lydia Mill baseball teams in 1921—they were undefeated. (Courtesy of Sam Owens.)

CLINTON MILL BASEBALL. This was one of the early Clinton Mill baseball teams in the late 1920s. (Courtesy of Clinton Mills.)

"My Dad." Baseball player Hall King was, through the eyes of his son, a "Big Leaguer." King was a supervisor of the Lydia Mill warehouse. (Courtesy of Clothmaker.)

Bell Street State Champs. Edd Little coached this team to the only state championship in the school history. (Courtesy of Monty Dutton.)

PENNANT WINNERS. The Clinton Cavaliers won first place in the Central Carolina League. Pictured, from left to right, are (front row) Lonie Lyles, Ellis Huffstetler, Frankie Aravelo, Bill Rowland, and Claude Crocker (manager); (middle row) Ralph Harbin, Charles Burnette, Guy Prater, Ralph Blackstop, and Zeb Eaton; (back row) Roy Whitaker, Mickey Livingston, Ott Thomas (bus driver), Charley Gaffney, and Pete Mish. (Courtesy of Sam Owens.)

LAST OF THE CAVALIERS. Pictured is the last Cavalier baseball team at Clinton Mills in 1961. Seen from left to right are (front row) Bill Sease, Fred Satterfield, Sam Owens, Jim Braswell, William Archie, and Bill Dobbins; (back row) Manager Truman Owens, Glen McGee, Tot Fallaw, Kinard Littleton, Earl Satterfield, and Rudy Hamrick. J.B. Vanderford was a member but is not pictured. (Courtesy of Sam Owens.)

CLINTON MILL BAND. This band was organized from Clinton Mills and entertained the community. They are pictured in 1917. (Courtesy of Clinton Mills.)

CLINTON DIXIE YOUTH. This 1954 Dixie Youth team was coached by Mr. D.S. Templeton and Charles Chuck Leatherwood. On the front row, second from the left, is Kinard Littleton, who went on to sign a Major League Baseball contract. (Courtesy of Sam Owens.)

CLARENCE EDWARD "CHICK" GALLOWAY. Chick Galloway became famous when he was named the American League's most valuable player in 1922. (Courtesy of Marsha Collection.)

BROADWAY THEATER. The new Broadway Theater replaced the old theater that opened in 1933. This theater was located on North Broad Street in Clinton and was built in 1950. (Courtesy of Sam Owens.)

www.ingramcontent.com/pod-product-compliance
Lightning Source LLC
Chambersburg PA
CBHW080854100426
42812CB00007B/2021